In the Ghettos

Teens Who Survived the
Ghettos of the Holocaust

Baltic
Sea

LITHUANIA
Kovno ★   ★ Vilna

★ Szarkowszczyzna

Bialystok ★   ★ Marcinkance   ★ Glebokie

BELARUS

(German-Occupied)
POLAND

□ Treblinka   ★ Minsk

Chelmno □

Warsaw ★   ■ Minsk
Mazowiecki   ★ Mir

★ Kopyl
Lachowicze ★

Lodz ★   Markuszow ★   Kletz ★   ★ Nesvizh

★ Lachva

GERMANY

Kruszyna ■   Kieke ★   □ Sobibor
Lublin-
Lipowa ■

Czestochowa ★
Bedzin ★   Radom ★   ★ Serniki

Sosnowiec ★

★ Pilica   ■ Janowska
(Lvov)   ★ Tuchin   UKRAINE

★ Krakow   ★ Ostrog

Auschwitz □   ★ Rogatin   ★ Kremenets

★ Proskurov

CZECHOSLOVAKIA

AUSTRIA

HUNGARY

ROMANIA

★ Ghettos
■ Labor Camps
□ Extermination Camps

In the Ghettos

Teens Who Survived the Ghettos of the Holocaust

Eleanor H. Ayer

THE ROSEN PUBLISHING GROUP, INC.
NEW YORK

Published in 1999 by The Rosen Publishing Group, Inc.
29 East 21st Street, New York, New York 10010

First Edition

Library of Congress Cataloging-in-Publication Data

Ayer, Eleanor H..
    In the ghettos : teens who survived the ghettos of the Holocaust / Eleanor H. Ayer.
    p.   cm.—(Teen witnesses to the Holocaust)
Includes bibliographical references and index.
    Summary: Chronicles the deportation of Jews into ghettos during Hitler's Third Reich and presents the narratives of three individuals who, as teenagers, lived in the ghettos of Lodz, Theresienstadt, and Warsaw and survived physical deprivations, abuse, and deportation to the death camps.
  ISBN 0-8239-2845-4
  1. Jewish children in the Holocaust—Biography—Juvenile literature. 2. Holocaust, Jewish (1939–1945)—Personal narratives—Juvenile literature. [1 Holocaust, Jewish (1939–1945)—Personal narratives. 2. Jews—Biography.] I. Title. II. Series.
D804.195.A94 1999
940.53'18'0835—dc21   98-43859
                                                           CIP
                                                           AC

Manufactured in the United States of America

Contents

Introduction

It is important for everyone to learn about the Holocaust, the systematic murder of 6 million Jews during World War II (1939–1945). It is a dark scar across the face of human history. As a student, you are part of the future generation that will lead and guide the family of humankind. Your proper understanding of the Holocaust is essential. You will learn its lessons. You will be able to ensure that a Holocaust will never happen again and that the world will be a safe place for each person—regardless of his or her nationality, religion, or ethnicity.

Nazi Germany added a dangerous new element to the familiar concept of "dislike of the unlike." The Nazis introduced the idea that an *ethnic group* whom someone dislikes or hates can be isolated from the rest of the population and earmarked for total destruction, *without any possibility of survival.*

The Nazis chose the Jewish people for this fatal annihilation. Their definition of a Jew was a uniquely racial one: a person with Jewish blood. To the Nazis, a person with even one Jewish grandparent was a Jew—a person to be killed.

The Germans systematically rounded up Jews in the countries that they occupied during World War II. They built death camps equipped with the most sophisticated technology available in order to kill the Jews. With the assistance of collaborators (non-Germans who willingly helped), they murdered more than 6 million Jews. Among the victims were 1.5 million children and teenagers. These Jewish children, like Jewish adults, had no options. They were murdered because they had

Two destitute children in the Warsaw ghetto, around 1941–1942.

Jewish blood, and nothing they could do could change that.

Such a thing had never happened before in recorded history, despite the fact that genocide (deliberate destruction of people of one ethnic, political, or cultural group) had occurred. In the past, victims or oppressed people were usually offered an option to avoid death: they could change their religion, or be expelled to another country. But the Nazi concept of racism did not give the victim any possibility for survival, since a person cannot change his or her blood, skin color, or eye color.

A few non-Jewish people, known as the Righteous Among the Nations, saved Jews from death. They felt that they were their brothers' and sisters' keepers. But they were in the minority. The majority were collaborators or bystanders. During the Holocaust, I was a young child saved by several Righteous Poles. The majority of my family and the Jews of my town, many of whose families had lived there for 900 years, were murdered by the Nazis with the assistance of local collaborators. Photographs of those who were murdered gaze upon visitors to the Tower of Life exhibit that I created for the United States Holocaust Memorial Museum in Washington, D.C.

We must learn the lessons of the Holocaust. We must learn to respect one another, regardless of differences in religion, ethnicity, or race, since we all belong to the family of humankind. The United States and Canada are both countries of immigrants, populated by many ethnic groups. In lands of such diversity, dislike of the unlike—the Nazi idea of using racial classification as a reason to destroy other humans—is dangerous to all of us. If we allow intolerance toward one group of people today, any of us could be part of a group selected for destruction tomorrow. Understanding and respecting one another regardless of religion, race, or ethnicity, is essential for coexistence and survival.

In this book individuals who were teenagers during the Holocaust share their experiences of life before and during the war and of the days of liberation. Their messages about their families, friends, love, suffering, survival, liberation, and rebuilding of new lives are deeply inspiring. They are important because these survivors are among the last eyewitnesses, the last links to what happened during the Holocaust.

I hope that their stories will encourage you to build a better, safer future "with liberty and justice for all."

Yaffa Eliach, Ph.D.
Professor of History and Literature
Department of Judaic Studies, Brooklyn College

7

chapter one

As dawn broke on September 1, 1939, German armies invaded Poland in a surprise attack. It was the start of World War II. Before the war ended in 1945, more than 50 million people were dead. Six million of them were Jews murdered by the Germans.

The Jews were murdered according to a plan created by German dictator Adolf Hitler and his Nazi Party. The plan was called the Final Solution. Its purpose was to "eliminate" the nine million Jews of Europe. The Nazis came close to achieving this goal. They rounded up the Jews and set up ghettos and concentration camps across the Reich—the vast area occupied by Germany. In the camps and ghettos, most Jews were executed or died of starvation, disease, and exhaustion.

Many of them were teens. This book relates the story of a few of those who survived.

The Beginning of the Ghettos

On September 20, 1939, three weeks after the start of the war, the Nazis issued an order. From that point on, all Jews living in countries under German control were required to move to special areas of large cities, called ghettos. As the Nazis invaded and occupied much

Jews entering the ghetto with their possessions await a search by German police.

of Europe, they created ghettos in all major European cities with Jewish populations. Since more than half the Jews of Europe lived in Poland and Eastern Europe, most of the ghettos were located there.

Once the Jews had been confined in ghettos and isolated from the rest of society, it was easier for the Nazis to put the Final Solution into effect. Thousands of Jews were murdered in mass killings or died of starvation, disease, and abuse inside the ghetto walls. Hundreds of thousands more were eventually loaded onto trains that carried them to Nazi death camps, where most were murdered.

The Nazis treated the Jews of the ghettos with unimaginable cruelty. Nazi soldiers were aware of their reputation for brutality, even boastful of it. A Nazi joke of the time suggests that they relished the power they wielded in the ghettos—and how they used it cruelly:

In the Warsaw ghetto a German soldier with a glass eye came to take a Jewish child from its mother. The mother begged him to spare the child. "If you can guess which of my eyes is artificial," said the soldier, "I'll give you your child."

After staring at the soldier a minute, the woman chose his right eye. "That's so," responded the surprised soldier, "but how could you tell?"

"Because," said the woman after a long pause, "it looks more human than the other."

A boy in the Warsaw ghetto huddles by the wall of a house.

chapter two

The Ghettos

In June 1941, the German army invaded Latvia, a country on the Baltic Sea that was then part of the Soviet Union. The Nazis set up a ghetto for Jews in the city of Libau (called Liepaja in Latvian) and used the ghetto inmates—thousands of men, women, and teenagers—as slave laborers. By the end of the summer, most of Libau's Jews had been murdered, most in mass executions in which Jews were rounded up and shot. The bodies of those executed were piled in one large grave or pit.

It was not always the Germans who murdered them. Many non-Jews in German-occupied lands were antisemitic, and they treated their Jewish neighbors savagely. They helped the Nazis kill Jews and even organized some of the mass murders. More than once, they set fire to synagogues with dozens of Jews trapped inside.

The Move to the Ghettos

The Libau ghetto was one of hundreds of ghettos set up by the Germans during the Holocaust. By Nazi order, every Jew in German-controlled lands had to live in a community of at least 500 people.

The bodies of Latvian Jews murdered by Latvian collaborators, June 1941.

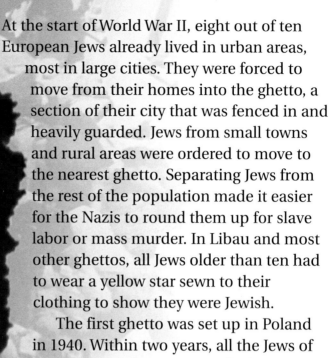

At the start of World War II, eight out of ten European Jews already lived in urban areas, most in large cities. They were forced to move from their homes into the ghetto, a section of their city that was fenced in and heavily guarded. Jews from small towns and rural areas were ordered to move to the nearest ghetto. Separating Jews from the rest of the population made it easier for the Nazis to round them up for slave labor or mass murder. In Libau and most other ghettos, all Jews older than ten had to wear a yellow star sewn to their clothing to show they were Jewish.

The first ghetto was set up in Poland in 1940. Within two years, all the Jews of Poland and the Nazi-controlled sections of the Soviet Union were in hiding, living in ghettos, trying to flee, or dead.

Ghettos in Every Major City

After the Germans invaded Poland in 1939, they began planning to set up Jewish ghettos there. The first permanent ghetto was established in Lodz in early 1940. Within months, Lublin, Radom, Lvov, and most other large Polish cities had ghettos. The ghettos were established quickly and without warning. The Nazis knocked on the doors of Jewish homes and gave the residents only minutes to gather their belongings and get out. Jews were then thrown into trucks or forced to walk to the ghetto. Their homes, with all their remaining possessions, were seized by the Nazis.

Few Gentiles, or non-Jews, in Eastern Europe did anything to

A child sells armbands on the street in the Warsaw ghetto.

stop the Germans' abuse of the Jews. In fact, many of them helped. Some helped out of fear that their own lives would be threatened if they did not. Others hoped to be rewarded with money or valuables. Many hated the Jews as much as the Nazis did.

According to the Nazis, the Poles too were an "inferior" people, worthy only of enslavement. In some Polish cities, the Germans forced Polish non-Jews from their homes into designated areas of the city and treated them in nearly the same inhumane manner.

After the Invasion

Rita Hilton was born in Warsaw, Poland, in 1926, and grew up near the city of Lodz. Her mother and grandfather were dentists who opened a practice together. Rita's life before the war was happy. She lived in a comfortable neighborhood with her mother, grandfather, and grandmother. She recalls how her town and the townspeople changed after the German invasion.

When the Germans occupied our town, they put a bunch of restrictions on Jews. We couldn't use the street cars. We couldn't use the cafe downstairs where everybody used to sit. We couldn't go to the park. Jewish schools were closed. . . . There were scenes downstairs: through the window I would see them grab a Jew and cut off his beard. And usually it was young kids doing it. They were like a bunch of little puppies jumping on people. This was the beginning.

We knew we would not be able to stay in our apartment. We lived in a fancy section of town, and it was a very large apartment. We kind of waited, wondering when they [the Germans] would kick us out. Sure enough, the order came: in twenty-four hours we had to leave behind bedding for twelve beds, all the china, all the furniture, all the equipment in the dental office. Everything had to be left. We were allowed to take only our personal clothing. That's when we moved to the Pabianice ghetto.

A Pole, he promised us that the ghetto would be just outside of town, a little suburban area, very quiet. Nothing would happen to us. In the ghetto, we had been told, Jews were not allowed to have money, only a limited amount of German marks—no gold, no silver, no diamonds. The Pole persuaded my grandfather that he would hold everything for safekeeping, he'd safeguard all of his valuables. Grandfather had all his money in a gold money belt. His total life savings was in those gold coins. American dollars, British sterling—everything in gold. He left it with the Pole.

After the ghetto was formed, we couldn't get out, but we sent someone to pick up my grandfather's money belt. The Pole denied that he had ever had it.

Structure of the Ghettos

The ghettos were horribly overcrowded. Entire families lived in a single room in a rundown building. Dozens of other families lived in adjoining rooms. Plumbing systems were broken, and electricity often did not work. Buildings had no heat. The Nazis made life unbearably brutal.

A Jewish council, or Judenrat, was put in charge of governing each ghetto. The Nazis chose the Jews who would serve on this council. The Judenrat had to organize sanitation systems, food and water distribution, jobs, welfare, heat, medical services, and police forces. It was an impossible job because the Nazis made sure that the ghettos always had shortages of food, heat, and health services. Council members got some special privileges for themselves and their families. But they paid dearly for them. When the Nazis ordered a deportation to a death camp, Judenrat members had to provide the list of names showing who would be deported. Sending fellow Jews to their deaths was a terrible burden for Judenrat members.

The Ghettos Are Sealed

At first, Polish cities such as Radom, Chelm, and Kielce had "open ghettos." Residents could pass from the ghetto into other parts of the city at specified times. Polish and German non-Jews could enter and leave the ghetto as they pleased. Rita recalls the Pabianice ghetto:

Pabianice was an open ghetto. There was... no barbed wire, just

Basic Services in the Ghettos

Every ghetto had a post office, but mail
was censored by the Nazis. Messages could
be written only in Polish or German.
Ghetto residents used postcards most
often, since they were more likely to get
past the censors.
No telephones or radios were allowed in
the ghettos. All were removed by order of
the Germans. Special money was printed for
use only in the ghetto, but it was
worthless compared to German money. Even
in the ghetto, it could buy very little.
Most ghettos had no courts or judges.

A five-mark note that was issued in the Lodz ghetto
by the local Judenrat, or Jewish Council.

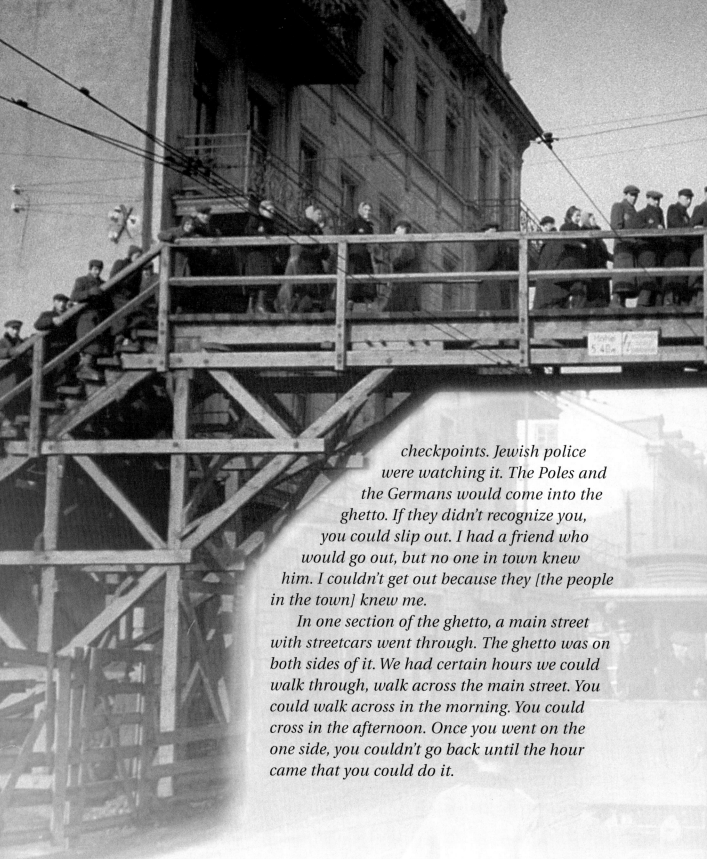

checkpoints. Jewish police were watching it. The Poles and the Germans would come into the ghetto. If they didn't recognize you, you could slip out. I had a friend who would go out, but no one in town knew him. I couldn't get out because they [the people in the town] knew me.

In one section of the ghetto, a main street with streetcars went through. The ghetto was on both sides of it. We had certain hours we could walk through, walk across the main street. You could walk across in the morning. You could cross in the afternoon. Once you went on the one side, you couldn't go back until the hour came that you could do it.

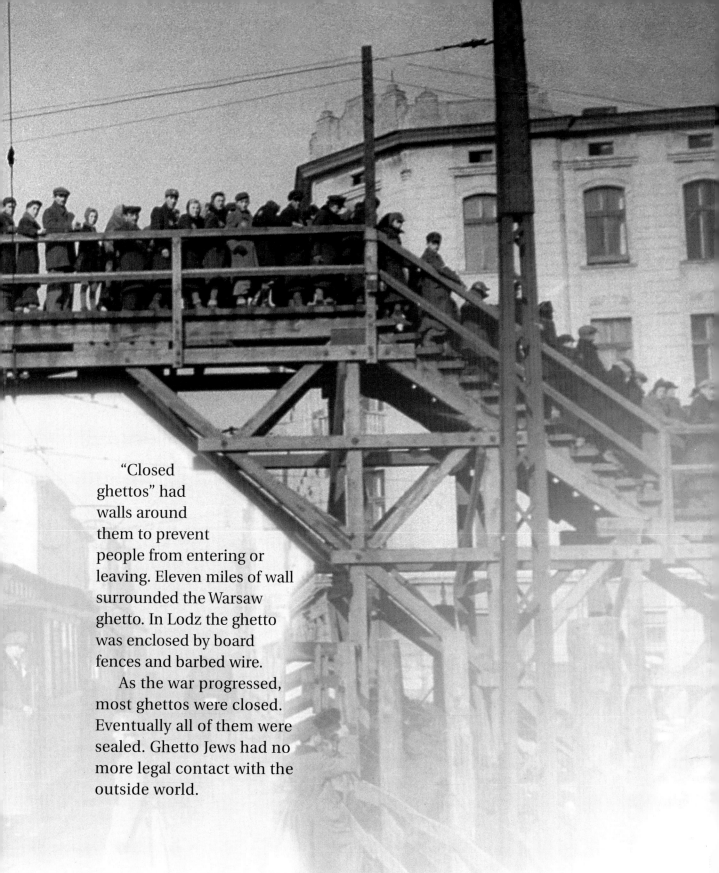

"Closed ghettos" had walls around them to prevent people from entering or leaving. Eleven miles of wall surrounded the Warsaw ghetto. In Lodz the ghetto was enclosed by board fences and barbed wire.

As the war progressed, most ghettos were closed. Eventually all of them were sealed. Ghetto Jews had no more legal contact with the outside world.

Prisoners of the Lodz ghetto walk across a bridge that segregated them from trolley car riders below. Lodz, Poland 1941.

chapter three

Condition in the Ghettos

Rita Hilton recalls the date—May 15 or 16, 1942—when she and her family were moved from the Pabianice ghetto. Ghetto residents were given just a couple of days to get ready. They were not told where they were being sent.

The Germans announced that a group of men would stay and work in the coat factories in the ghetto. They also selected a group of people who would stay in the ghetto and clean it up. And they needed medical personnel also. Everyone else was told to bring all the infirm—all the sick ones, all the very old ones—to the hospital. Our family was ordered to go to the hospital, too, because there were a lot of patients to be seen. . . .

On the day the ghetto was emptied, we were allowed to take just what we had on our backs and in our bundles. We wore a few layers of clothes to the hospital. When we got to the hospital, we were told that there was an old age home in town. We carried the patients from there, whoever was left, to the hospital.

That same day, the Germans marched the rest of the population of the ghetto to the stadium at the other end of town. We were in the

Jewish deportees from the Lodz ghetto, who have just been transferred from a closed passenger train to a train of open cattle cars, on their way to the Chelmno death camp. Kolo, Poland, 1942.

hospital that night, so we didn't see what happened, but we found out about it the next day.

As they approached the stadium, there was an area that was fenced off. There the Nazis started separating the parents, the old ones, and they started taking the children away, all the children under ten years old. I was told that they threw a baby over the fence and said, "We don't need such ___." They mashed the baby's head on a fence. They took all of tbe old people and children to the railroad station. Later that night, they took all the women who were left to Lodz.

The following day some boys who were friends of ours came to the hospital. They told us that the Germans were putting people into cattle cars, and that they had taken the women to Lodz by streetcar. Just the men were left in the stadium. These men carried the patients out of the hospital and to the carts, and they announced that whoever couldn't walk should go on a cart.

My grandmother felt that she couldn't walk all the way. I think this was Sunday, because a lot of people were there, and some of them would make the sign of the cross when they recognized us. . . .

You had to turn left to get to the stadium. The train station was straight ahead. All the carts with the patients went straight, and the cart with the boys went straight, and then we kind of froze for a minute—and the cart with my grandmother and other people went left, to the stadium.

Those on the cart that went straight were put in cattle cars and deported to a death camp, but Rita did not know that at the time.

That night the Nazis took us to Lodz by streetcar. The streetcars stopped running about midnight, and that's when they were taking us all to the Lodz ghetto. That second day, it was just men and our group from the hospital. I think that out of a population of 8,000, finally 3,000 or 3,500 wound up in the Lodz ghetto.

She recalls her family's life in the Lodz ghetto.

We started our existence. I wouldn't call it living, in the Lodz ghetto. Conditions were horrid. We had one room, which was our bedroom, our living room, our kitchen, our bathroom. The first few nights, Mom and I slept on a straw mattress on the floor, and mice came in and started running on our faces, so we had to give this up. We shared one bed, and Grandma had a cot, and Grandfather had a bed.

We had cold water only. We had to pump the water from downstairs to bring it up. And they had laundries, public laundries. You sent out your stuff, it took three months, two months, you got it back. Not that we had valuable things.

We all worked. The head of the Lodz ghetto didn't like dentists, so my mother worked as a nurse in one of the factories. I worked in a brassiere factory. Grandfather worked as a male nurse in one of the factories. Grandma got a job sorting rags and making balls of those colored rags, which were eventually used to make rugs for the Germans. The problem was that the rags were full of lice. So she was bringing the lice home.

Shortages

Hunger. Disease. Fuel shortages. Life in the ghetto was so wretched it was impossible to say which problem was the worst.

For teenagers, whose bodies were growing and demanding

A man and a boy wrestle over a piece of bread on a Warsaw ghetto street.

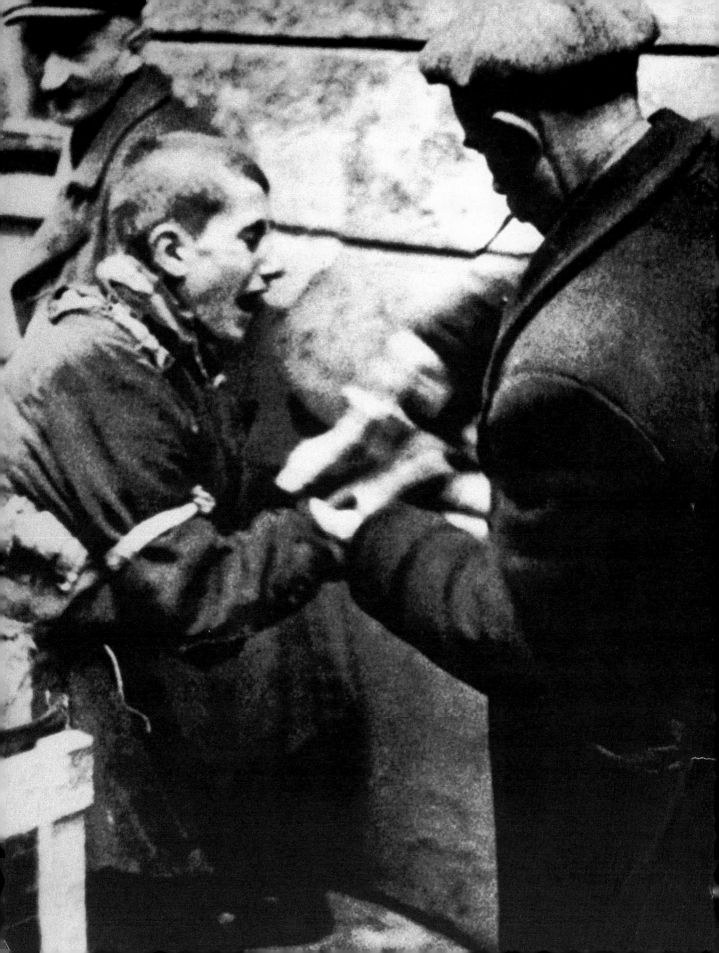

Smugglers in the Warsaw ghetto, winter 1940. Since food and other supplies were lacking in ghettos, smugglers helped keep ghetto residents alive.

nutrition, hunger was constant and overpowering. In the Warsaw ghetto, food was rationed by the Germans according to calories. An average person needs about 2,000 calories a day. Teenagers require more. But in the ghetto, Poles received 669 calories a day; Jews received 184. Even with the illegal smuggling of food into the ghetto, most people never got more than 1,100 calories per day.

With food so scarce, ghetto residents were forced to smuggle it in from the outside if they could. This was dangerous work. Smugglers caught by the Nazis were killed. Children and teenagers, who were nimble and often small, made some of the best smugglers. Not only did they bring back food, they also smuggled in newspapers, money, medicine, valuables with which to trade, and other goods that were lacking in the ghetto.

Disease and Death

Overcrowding, starvation, and cold led to health problems in the ghettos. Typhus—the deadly infectious disease that killed teenager

A boy who has fainted from hunger lies on the pavement in the ghetto. During January 1942, a typical month in the Lodz ghetto, 1,083 men and 704 women died from disease or hunger.

Anne Frank, author of the famous diary—was spread by lice and seemed to be everywhere. Because there was no hot water or soap, people could not keep their bodies free from lice.

Although typhus was the most widespread, other diseases killed more people. Heart disease brought on by high stress killed the greatest number of adults. Teenagers often died of tuberculosis, dysentery, intestinal problems, malnutrition, or exhaustion.

Death tolls were staggering. In the Warsaw ghetto alone, between November 1940 and April 1943, 100,000 Jews died from hunger or disease. This did not include the thousands more who were deported to Nazi death camps.

Finding the Will to Live

With death a constant companion in the ghetto, it was all too easy to think of suicide. Fortunately, most Jews in the ghettos had a strong determination to live. Many found ways to maintain the

The Constant, Gripping Cold

Emmanuel Ringelblum was a Jewish historian who kept a diary throughout his stay in the Warsaw ghetto. In mid-November 1941, he wrote that the worst sight was that of the freezing children. "They whine, beg, sing, lament and tremble in the cold, without underwear, without clothes, without shoes, covered only by rags and bags which are tied by strings to meager skeletons." These were not just young children. Many older teenagers also stood in rags, looking like living skeletons.

The Jews in the ghettos of Eastern Europe froze because the Germans had confiscated their winter clothing and shipped it back to Germany, to be given to German soldiers or citizens. Going indoors did little to keep the Jews warm, for there was no fuel for heating. In the Warsaw ghetto, coal was so scarce it was called "black pearls."

In Lodz, ghetto officials allowed people to tear down unused wooden buildings and burn the wood for fuel. One official told how people moved in "like crows on a cadaver, like jackals on a carcass. They demolished, they axed, they sawed, walls collapsed, beams flew, plaster buried people alive, but no one yielded his position."

A boy in the Warsaw ghetto, September 19, 1941. His jacket is made entirely out of scraps that were stitched together and that have again split in many places. He was lucky compared to some children who had only thin jackets and not even a single shoe.

communities' spirit. This spirit kept many from killing themselves.

Humor helped the Jews to keep their sanity. They told jokes and made up songs. Not surprisingly, many of the jokes were political. If the Nazis had heard them, it would have meant torture or death. One song urged:

Let's be joyous and tell our jokes
We'll hold a wake when Hitler chokes

The Nazis banned religious services in most ghettos and destroyed synagogues. But this did not keep people from praying. They gathered in one another's homes to celebrate the holidays and holy days. For a time, they even observed the Sabbath as a day of rest. Living under so much stress, many people's faith grew stronger.

Having the support of a family was another great boost to the spirit. This was not easy to maintain. Death and deportation often separated family members. For families who stayed together, tensions caused by hunger, misery, and stress made it hard for people to get along with each other. Still, supportive families gave people a stronger will to live.

In addition, ghetto teenagers banded together in youth groups. Most were political. Members issued announcements and bulletins about ghetto activities and news of the war. They held secret meetings where they openly discussed ideas forbidden by the Nazis. They read banned books and newspapers that had been smuggled into the ghetto.

Ghetto youth groups were sometimes in contact with resistance groups outside the ghetto. Resistance groups were made up of people secretly opposed to the Nazis. Sometimes couriers in the Resistance managed to relay news from ghetto to ghetto. These couriers created a patchy communications network, allowing residents in one ghetto to know what was occurring elsewhere. Another important source of information was the workers who went out of the ghetto during the day to work. They could sometimes gather information from people on the outside.

Morning prayer at a former synagogue in the Warsaw ghetto in April 1940. At that time, the building served as living quarters for Jews deported from Lodz and other places.

A poetry class at the Warsaw ghetto boarding school for boys. The Yiddish poem on the blackboard is by A. Reizen. Warsaw, June 5, 1940.

In Search of a "Normal" Life

Despite the horror all around them, people in the ghetto tried to brighten up their lives with cultural activities. Since the Nazis did not allow these activities in most ghettos, residents had to do them in secret.

Libraries were set up in some ghettos, allowing teens and children a brief escape into books. Concerts and performances were held. Inmates put on plays and performed puppet shows for children. There were art exhibits and readings by poets and writers.

Schools were set up in some of the ghettos. Despite starvation and disease, unheated classrooms, and few textbooks or supplies, children flocked to these schools. It was a relief to be away from the misery of home and the horror of people dying in the streets.

Soon the Nazis made it illegal to hold classes. To get around this, ghetto organizers disguised schools as soup kitchens or workshops.

An adult would gather a few students in his or her home and teach them Hebrew, mathematics, literature, or other subjects. If a Nazi suddenly showed up, the teacher would pick up a shoe or piece of cloth and behave as if he or she were training the children how to mend shoes, sew, or learn some other trade important to the Reich.

By late 1941, Lodz and certain other ghettos forced children age ten and older to work. This ended all hope of getting an education—unless the children could find a way to do it on their own.

Between 1940 and 1942, the Nazis established hundreds of ghettos in Poland and elsewhere in Eastern Europe. Each had its own rules and a unique character. Three of the most famous were the Lodz and Warsaw ghettos in Poland, and Theresienstadt in Czechoslovakia. The Lodz ghetto, established early in 1940, was the first ghetto the Nazis created. The Warsaw ghetto, which was the largest, became famous because its residents fought the Germans, with some success. Theresienstadt was used as a Nazi showplace to trick foreign inspectors into believing that the ghettos, though confining, were decent places to live.

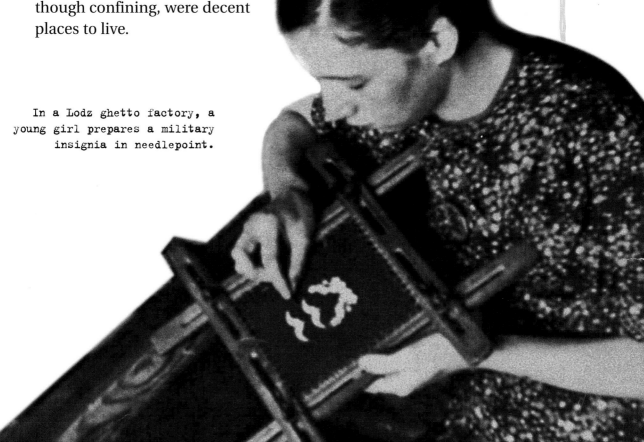

In a Lodz ghetto factory, a young girl prepares a military insignia in needlepoint.

chapter four

The Lodz Ghetto

Lodz was the second-largest ghetto in Poland, at one point housing approximately 164,000 people. It lasted longer than any other ghetto; it wasn't liquidated (emptied of people) until summer 1944.

On May 1, 1940, the Lodz ghetto was officially sealed. A fence of wood and barbed wire was built around it. Armed guards patrolled its borders. They had orders to shoot anyone who came near. Unlike some ghettos, Lodz was truly isolated. So tightly was it sealed that no help, not even from the Resistance, could get in from the outside.

Unlike Warsaw and other ghettos, where upper, middle, and lower classes existed as they had in the rest of society, there were no class distinctions in Lodz. No one was given special privileges. Everyone was treated equally. Teenagers in the youth movements helped to make this happen. They encouraged people to share food rations and work duties imposed by the Nazis and to take risks equally. When someone needed help or food, everyone pitched in.

There were more German officials in Lodz than in most other ghettos. Nazis were everywhere, checking on the Judenrat, on the factory workers, on people in their homes and in the streets. One reason for this close observation was the ghetto's huge sewing industry. The Lodz ghetto produced clothing and uniforms vital to the German war effort.

Rita Hilton remembers how people in the Lodz ghetto worked.

The ghetto was one huge factory, starting from electronic equipment, uniforms, which were the most important things, boots, supplies for the army, going down to the brassieres, hats, artificial flowers, brooms, and even those rag rugs, braided rugs which were made out of scraps. They would take torn sheets that they would get when other towns or cities were liquidated. So everybody was working and everybody who produced something was getting food.

King Chaim of Lodz

Another reason for the heavy German presence in the Lodz ghetto was the Nazis' uneasiness with Mordechai Chaim Rumkowski. Rumkowski ran the Lodz ghetto's Judenrat from 1940 until the ghetto was liquidated in 1944. He was a strong leader, but not always well-liked among the Jews. Rumkowski wanted to make Lodz an independent, self-sufficient ghetto. He believed (correctly) that people would rather work than be idle.

As the working and living conditions in the ghetto grew steadily worse, Rumkowski's lust for power grew. He treated his workers harshly to make himself look better among the Germans. For this reason, many people began calling him "King Chaim." Soon he began calling people and places in the ghetto, "my Jews, my houses,

Chaim Rumkowski visits an orphanage in Lodz during the Jewish holiday of Purim, 1942. A few months later, these children were deported to death camps.

A woman and child kiss through the fence at the central prison in the
Lodz ghetto on the eve of a deportation of children and old people to
Chelmno death camp, September 1942.

my factories, my bread."

Rumkowski had control over "his Jews" and over the day-to-day
workings of the ghetto, but he had no power to stop the Nazis from
deporting Jews from Lodz to the death camps. After learning of a
deportation planned for early September 1942, he had to deliver
terrible news at a meeting in the ghetto:

"The ghetto has taken a grievous blow. They [the Nazis] have
asked us for the ghetto's most precious people: the children and the
elderly. I devoted my best years to children. I lived and breathed with
them. I never imagined that my hands would be forced to [kill
them]."

Rita Hilton was not much older than the children Rumkowski was
forced to send to their deaths. Rita passed her sixteenth birthday
shortly after she and her family were deported to the Lodz ghetto.

Opposite page: Four children haul a heavily laden cart through the
streets of the Lodz ghetto, 1942.

"They were evacuating people constantly," Rita recalled.

One of the worst actions was when they took the children out. Orders came that they have to take the children, they're going to take them to better places. There will be fresh air and farms. The people put up signs, and they mobilized all the Jewish police, including all the people who worked for the health department, and my mother, and they had to go and collect the children. The children were being taken voluntarily by the parents, taken down because they couldn't hide them. The moment the family would hide a child, rations would be taken away, so not only the child didn't have rations; the family wouldn't have rations.

Then they were taking the old people. They would make everyone line up on the street and just select the old people and the children.

Nearly 15,000 people—children, people who were in poor health, and old people—were swept away in the September 1942 deportation. For the first time, ghetto residents saw the truth. People who were deported were not "resettled" in the east, as the Germans said they would be. They were murdered. Why else would children and old people, who were useless for work, be deported?

Grim Life in Lodz

Two years after the September deportation, Rita narrowly escaped a roundup, or *Aktion*, in her neighborhood. Thanks to Rita's landlady, all the people in Rita's building escaped the roundup. The Germans had ordered people on a certain street to line up outside.

Children are transported on horse-drawn wagons to an assembly point during a roundup, or *Aktion*, in the Lodz ghetto. From there, the children, along with the infirm and the aged, were deported to the Chelmno death camp. Lodz, September 10, 1942.

We lived on a corner. Our so-called landlady was the wife of a guy who had been killed. We started lining up on one street, and the landlady called out to everybody and said, "Forget it. This is not our street. Our address is the next street." There were two entrances to the building, one on one street and one around the corner on the other. She said, "All of you go back home and hide. Just sit quiet, don't open the window, don't stand next to windows." At that time she had hidden some children and my grandparents. We didn't know where they were, somewhere. They had all kinds of nooks and crannies in that building, and we had all hidden quietly. At noon the Germans blew the whistles, and they stopped the Aktion. *So, just when they were ready to call that second street, where we were, they called it off, and we were saved. It was terrifying.*

Although Rita and her family were temporarily spared from the deportations, they suffered the effects of their physical deprivation.

We all started getting sick. I was getting abscesses on my face and sties in my eyes. Grandfather fell on the ice and broke his arm, and he started staying in bed. Grandmother had dizzy spells.

My grandfather was getting weaker and weaker. He couldn't eat. This was really awful, so we kept on saving his bread. And his wish was to live long enough for us to pick up his next ration. This was his inheritance because, he said, he lost all his gold, and he can't leave us anything else.

He died the day before the rations came. We didn't report his death until the following day. We picked up his ration, and then I reported the death, so we had this extra little food and an extra loaf of bread.

Surviving Day by Day

Inmates in the ghettos had to be resourceful. For children and teens, having clothing that fit was the rarest of luxuries. Most, including Rita, struggled with ill-fitting shoes and too few clothes.

I was a young girl, and I didn't have any clothing, and we used every piece of scrap of whatever we could do something to make something.

I'll always remember an orange piece of fabric. It was not enough for a dress. I had a friend who was a dressmaker, and she said, "Find some wool." I found some on the black market, and she made me knit parts of the sleeves and the yoke and the turtleneck, and some trim on the skirt. She made pockets, and I had a beautiful dress made out of a very small piece of fabric and those scraps.

The Germans, too, were sparing in their use of materials. Many of the materials used in ghetto factories had been stolen from concentration camp inmates, who were ordered to remove their clothes just before they were gassed.

Deportation

Like thousands of other Lodz ghetto residents, Rita, her mother, and her grandmother were eventually deported. It was the beginning of August 1944.

There were about eighty people in the cattle car and one bucket, one slop bucket. I don't even know if there was anything to drink. We all had something to eat, whatever we'd grabbed. We had been saving bread because we were so conditioned that you have to save something for tomorrow.

People were dying on the train. There were all kinds of rumors but no one knew where we were going. We hadn't heard of Auschwitz. We had heard about bad things happening, but the only time that I knew something was happening was when those boys told us that the people were taken to cattle cars—the old people and the children—and those boys were never heard of again.

Rita, her mother, and her grandmother were deported from the Lodz ghetto to Auschwitz. Today, not a trace of the ghetto that they unwillingly called home remains.

chapter five

The Theresienstadt Ghetto

Forty miles north of Prague, Czechoslovakia, is the town of Terezin. There, on November 24, 1941, the Nazis established the Theresienstadt ghetto.

Terezin was an old, walled town where military troops and their families had once lived. It had more than two hundred two-story houses and fourteen huge stone barracks. When the Jewish deportees arrived, nearly sixty thousand people were crowded into a space designed to house seven thousand people.

Men and women were separated. At first, children under twelve stayed with their mothers. Teenagers went with the parent of their own sex. Later, all young people were housed in separate barracks called "children's homes." Those too young to work were cared for by older children and female supervisors.

Theresienstadt was unlike other ghettos. It was not a poor section of town to which local Jews were herded. It was more like a concentration camp. Jews were shipped there from all parts of the Reich. Teenagers fourteen and older did the same types of labor as adults.

An aerial view of Theresienstadt, the Nazis' "model camp."

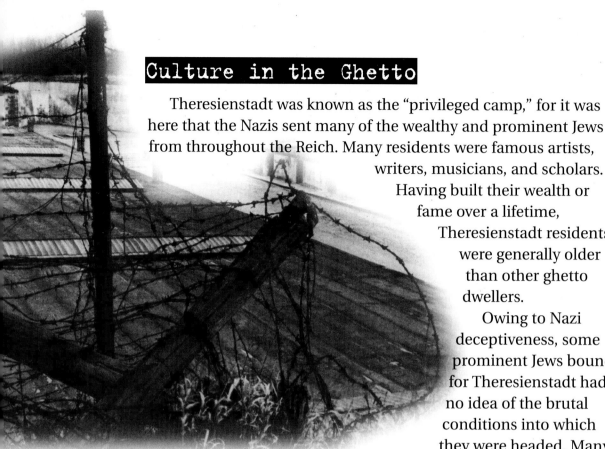

Culture in the Ghetto

Theresienstadt was known as the "privileged camp," for it was here that the Nazis sent many of the wealthy and prominent Jews from throughout the Reich. Many residents were famous artists, writers, musicians, and scholars. Having built their wealth or fame over a lifetime, Theresienstadt residents were generally older than other ghetto dwellers.

Owing to Nazi deceptiveness, some prominent Jews bound for Theresienstadt had no idea of the brutal conditions into which they were headed. Many wealthy Jews naively paid the Nazis large sums of money for special rooms with a good view. They arrived dressed in their best clothes, as if they had come to a resort. It soon became clear, however, that Theresienstadt was no better than any other concentration camp. The special treatment they had paid for was nothing but a scam.

While people were dying of disease, starvation, and exposure throughout most of Theresienstadt, culture was blooming in a section set aside by the Nazis as a showplace for visiting foreign officials. In this refined part of the ghetto, for a brief time, musicians formed orchestras and performed concerts. The lending library had more than sixty thousand books. There was a theater group with talented actors. Scholars and professors gave lectures. Artists painted and exhibited their pictures. Schools were set up for children and those teenagers who could be spared from work. Young people competed in athletic events. Most of these activities were unheard of in other ghettos.

View of the fourth courtyard of the Little Fortress in Theresienstadt, where executions were routinely carried out.

38

The artists, writers, and musicians knew that in public they were free to create and perform only what the Nazis approved. They did this during the day. At night, they produced their own works that told of the terrible existence at Theresienstadt.

Threshold to Auschwitz

Not only was Theresienstadt both a ghetto and a concentration camp, the Nazis also marked it as a transit camp. Jews were shipped from western and central Europe to Theresienstadt to await transport to the East. Most often, the transports went to Auschwitz.

The transports began in early 1942. Each train carried about one thousand people to the death camps in Poland. Only 1 percent—about ten people—survived each transport. The death rate for children was even higher. Of the 15,000 children under the age of fifteen who passed through Theresienstadt between 1942 and 1944, only about a hundred survived. Older teenagers stood a better chance. They were better able to care for themselves, and their young, strong bodies made them of value to the Reich as workers.

Too often, it didn't matter how able-bodied a person was. Old, young, weak, and strong were all sent East to be killed. Many prisoners weren't entirely sure where they were headed. But most had a dark feeling about the future.

The Beautification Project

The Germans called Theresienstadt their "model camp." Here they brought prominent visitors to show them how well the Germans treated their prisoners. No barbed wire surrounded Theresienstadt, just a high wall. Fewer Nazis patrolled the grounds than in other ghettos. It didn't look like a bad place.

But the look was all a front. In the fall of 1943, representatives from the

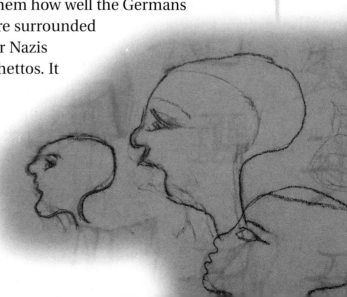

A drawing done by Eva Hesk during her internment at Theresienstadt, entitled *Heads*.

International Red Cross announced they would visit Theresienstadt. The Danish government wanted the Red Cross to check on the Danish Jews who had been deported there. For weeks before the visit, prisoners were worked like slaves to make the place look nice. This was called the "Beautification Project."

Inmates painted buildings and rooms to make them fresh and bright. They planted grass. New playground equipment was brought in for the children. The inmates built a soccer field, and young people began practicing. A children's play, *Brundibar,* featuring many teenage actors and crew members, was written just for the occasion.

A transport arriving in Theresienstadt.

Across the door of a building that was supposed to be a school hung a sign. It read: "CLOSED FOR THE HOLIDAYS." But the sign was permanent.

On the day of the visit, smartly dressed teenagers strolled the streets, buying fruit from sidewalk vendors and chatting in small groups. When the Red Cross inquired about life in Theresienstadt, they smiled and said it was fine. One of the soccer teams scored a goal, just as the visitors walked by. The Red Cross left with a good impression of how Germans treated their prisoners.

The minute the visitors were gone, the Nazis took back the nice

clothes. Lollipops that had been given to the children were snatched away. Toys disappeared. The soccer field again became a work area. And the life of deprivation at Theresienstadt returned.

The Little Fortress

Any prisoners who had not cooperated with the Beautification Project were taken to the Little Fortress. This was a prison located just outside of town. Conditions there were much worse than at Theresienstadt. Most prisoners were kept in solitary confinement. They lived under a constant threat of death. About two thousand were executed.

Two scenes from the performance of a play in *The Führer Gives the Jews a City*, a propaganda film that the Nazis made in Theresienstadt in 1944. Filming took place at the Sokol gymnasium, which until then prisoners had not been allowed to enter.

One person who came close to dying in the Little Fortress was Irene Weber, who had grown up in Sosnowiec, near the city of Katowice in western Poland. After the Nazis invaded her town in 1939, when she was ten or eleven years old, life became "very restricted," recalls Irene. The Germans assured residents that they would be much safer if they obtained working cards. Irene got her card and began work at a factory cutting thread. But the factory was raided by the Nazis, and Irene was taken to a concentration camp in the nearby town of Gleiwitz, on the German-Polish border. She did not see her family again.

Life continued to deteriorate for Irene until she eventually ended up in the very worst section of Theresienstadt, the Little Fortress.

Here she was sentenced to death through starvation.

We were put in a cell with about sixty women, and on the floor straw mattresses—very little straw and a lot of fleas—and one bathroom. There was a girl next to me who had been shot through her arm and her leg. She had gangrene. There was no medical help whatsoever. Nothing. Still, we helped one another. We tore our clothes and bandaged her wounds.

We were given rations—food—every other day. And you can imagine that being as hungry, as starved, as we were, it was very hard to ration this for two days. A slice of bread and some soup, without salt, for I suppose salt gives one some energy. There was one window in the cell, very high, and in the bathroom there was a little hole for air in the wall.

Somehow we established contact with Czechoslovakian prisoners who were working in the kitchen and on the grounds. Once every other day the guard opened the door and put some food in a barrel and a portion of bread for everyone. And somehow those prisoners slipped a piece of paper in there saying to tell them what we want and to put it through the hole in the bathroom wall. If anyone was sick, they would smuggle some aspirin to our cell.

Existence in this cell was pure hell. We were in very crowded conditions. The only way of cleansing our bodies was washing at the sink. We were bitten by fleas. We were hungry; we were starving. And there was no one. We were totally cut off from the outside world, except through that little hole in the wall.

I was there from January until May [1945], four months. The last days we had no food at all. But let me tell you something about our people. We did not steal. . . . from each other. We didn't. And the ill and weak and totally exhausted—we still cared for the ones that needed help a little more than we did. At one point I got very sick. I had a tonsillitis infection and a high fever. My friend was taking care of me. She didn't want to take my bread. I couldn't eat it. My tonsils were very swollen. I couldn't swallow. I had high fever. And I told her, "Please, you eat it, I can't have it. I can't swallow. You have it."

And she says, "No, Irene, I will keep it for you. I will save it for you. When you feel better, you will eat it." And she was starving herself.

Any one of the Germans—they performed acts of cruelty with such

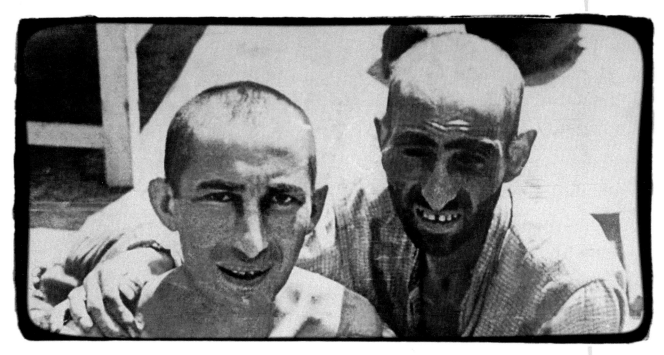

Two survivors of the Little Fortress at Theresienstadt, May 1945.

ease; they were killing with such ease; they were torturing with such ease that it's just unbelievable. And I thought, "If someday there were a [free] land and I will live, what will I make of it? How will I deal with people?" And then I said to myself, "I will deal with people well because I'm good. I didn't do anything wrong, and I couldn't do or feel the things that the Germans did." That kept me going, I think. That's why I survived and was able to function.

chapter six

The Warsaw Ghetto

Before the start of World War II, Warsaw, Poland's capital, had the largest Jewish population of any city in Europe. One-third—375,000—of Warsaw's residents were Jews. The city was a rich center of Jewish culture. All of that ended when the Germans invaded Poland in September 1939.

One month later, the Warsaw Judenrat was set up. On November 4, the SS (Hitler's security forces) gave orders to the Judenrat: All the Jews of Warsaw had three days to move into the ghetto. If they did not, members of the Judenrat would be shot. Thirty percent of the city's population was forced into a space made up of just 2.4 percent of the city's land. More than 120,000 people were squeezed into each square kilometer. As the months passed, more Jews were transported to the ghetto from elsewhere in Eastern Europe, until more than a half million people lived there.

Begging, Peddling, Smuggling

On November 16, 1940, the Warsaw ghetto was sealed. Overnight, conditions became much worse. Food was very scarce. No longer could people get supplies from outside the ghetto. Young people had to steal, beg, and smuggle food into the ghetto from the Polish part of the city in order to survive.

One of those was fifteen-year-old Icek Baum, the second of seven children. Baum had spent much of his early childhood in an orphanage, because his widowed mother could not afford to care for all the children. The orphanage was run by a physician and former teacher, Janusz Korczak, who was well-known to the children of Warsaw.

Janusz Korczak with his pupils in front of the children's home on Krochmalna Street in Warsaw, 1940.

"He was a terrific man," Baum recalls. "He was a very, very good man, and he kissed everybody. He had such a warm heart." Once the Warsaw ghetto was established, Dr. Korczak moved his orphanage there.

When the Germans began moving Warsaw Jews into the ghetto, the Baum family was among the first to be moved. Icek, who was away at summer camp, was not caught in the roundup. When he returned to Warsaw, he lived on the Polish side of the city, not in the ghetto. As long as he did not get caught, he was able to help his family. "My brothers, my sisters, my mother—they didn't have food, nothing to eat, absolutely nothing," Baum recalls.

So I know a man who is a butcher. He comes to me and asks if I want to make some money. "You have a face nobody can tell is a Jew's," he says to me. "You take meat. You go to the ghetto. You sell the meat. You help me, you help yourself. You can help your family."

So at a certain time every day, about 5:00 o'clock in the morning, when the first streetcar passes, I have my shoulder pack on my back, and I have meat. I don't remember how much exactly, maybe 25 kilos, 30 kilos (60 lbs.). And I have a Jewish armband with me. I have it in my pocket. When I am on the Polish side, I don't wear my band. I am a

A huge collection of records—diaries, reports, photos—were discovered in the Warsaw ghetto after the war. Its compilers called it the Oneg Shabbat—"Joy of the Sabbath." Warsaw ghetto residents led by historian Emanuel Ringelblum secretly put together these records hoping that the true history of the Warsaw ghetto would one day be known. They hid them from the Germans in milk cans and metal boxes that they buried in the ghetto.

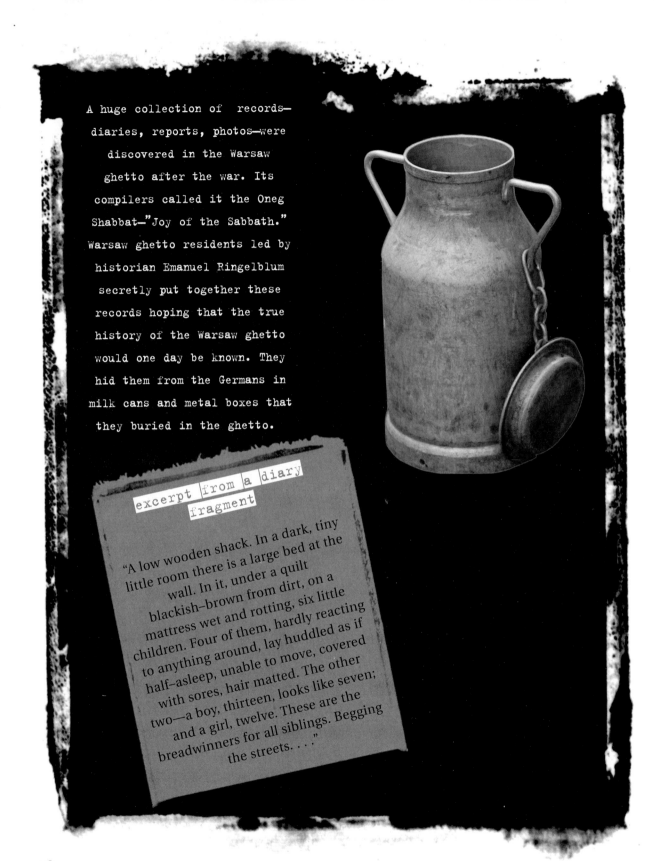

excerpt from a diary fragment

"A low wooden shack. In a dark, tiny little room there is a large bed at the wall. In it, under a quilt blackish–brown from dirt, on a mattress wet and rotting, six little children. Four of them, hardly reacting to anything around, lay huddled as if half–asleep, unable to move, covered with sores, hair matted. The other two—a boy, thirteen, looks like seven; and a girl, twelve. These are the breadwinners for all siblings. Begging the streets. . . ."

Polack. When I pass into the ghetto, I put my armband on, and I am a Jew.

The meat man tells me, "You put on your things and go to this and this address." But I say, "The Polish police, the police!"

"Don't worry," he says. "The policeman turns his back with his hand behind, and you push in some money, and he doesn't see, doesn't look at you." So I go in. The policeman was there with his hand behind his back, to see if I would give him some money. And when I sell the meat, I have some money. I go to my mother, give her the money.

```
  Janusz Korczak and Orphans
        in the Ghetto

Thousands of young people were made orphans
by the Nazis. In the Warsaw ghetto, Janusz
Korczak ran the orphanage. Under his care
were 192 children and teenagers. Korczak was
very devoted to these children. He protected
   them as best he could from Nazi terror.
     But on August 5, 1942, Korczak reached
the end of his ability. His children were
scheduled to be deported to the Treblinka
death camp. No one, he knew, ever returned
from Treblinka. Korczak pleaded with the
Judenrat to keep his orphans from being
deported. It did no good. Because he was a
physician, the Nazis offered to spare
Korczak's own life. They could use him
      elsewhere in the ghetto.
           He refused.
He insisted on going to his death with
           the children.
```

Icek witnessed firsthand the cruelty of the Nazis in the Warsaw ghetto.

Every time I come there, I see people lying outside starving. The Germans come in there laughing. They take all kinds of pictures of the poor people, and it is very, very hard to explain. The people are dead, all dead. You don't have nothing there. No food; cold. People are outside begging for pieces of bread, and some, they have children. The children sneak out through the wall to the Polish side to take something, to have some potatoes, and then they are chased by the Germans. The Germans kill them, they shoot them. I can't explain to you.

Defiant

For nearly two years, the Jews of Warsaw struggled to survive in the wretched ghetto conditions. Each month the transports to death camps carried away thousands of people. In the summer of 1942, rumors of a huge deportation—300,000 people—rocked the ghetto.

The Nazis ordered Adam Czerniakow, chairman of the Warsaw Judenrat, to oversee the deportation. All but 120,000 residents were to be transported. Czerniakow begged the Nazis to spare the children. But he was powerless before them. His request was denied. He grew frantic.

On July 23, Czerniakow decided he could no longer do the Nazis' horrible work. He swallowed a capsule of cyanide, a deadly poison, and was dead within minutes. The deportation of 300,000 Jews took place nonetheless.

By the fall of 1942, only about 55,000 people remained in the ghetto. It was then that the ghetto's ZOB, the Zydowska Organizacja Bojowa, or Jewish Fighting Organization, went into action.

The ZOB was a group of young people in their teens and early twenties. They vowed that they would not go to their deaths without a fight. Their leader, Mordecai Anielewicz, was twenty-three. The group was untrained in fighting and had few good weapons.

A debris-filled street in the Warsaw ghetto during the the ghetto uprising in 1943.

Nazi SS troops walk past a block of burning homes during the suppression of the Warsaw ghetto uprising. Only after twenty-eight days of fighting were the Nazis able to suppress the remarkable uprising.

But they were fighting for their lives, which gave them courage.

On January 9, 1943, Gestapo chief Heinrich Himmler ordered the deportation of another 8,000 Jews. This time, many ghetto residents who were on the list did not report to the trains. Instead, they went into hiding. When surprised Nazi troops tried to force them out by firing on them, the ŻOB fought back with crude weapons. Finally the Germans left. But everyone knew they would be back.

The Warsaw Ghetto Uprising

On April 19, 1943, during the Jewish holiday of Passover, the uprising began. At 6:00 AM, two thousand German soldiers with tanks and flamethrowers entered the ghetto. They intended to force out the Jews who remained and put them on transports to death camps. The ŻOB had only a few guns and homemade weapons. But they had fierce determination.

For a remarkable twenty-eight days, the young people of the Warsaw ghetto bravely fought the well-supplied and well-fed German forces. It was a milestone in Jewish history. For centuries, their culture and religion had taught them to negotiate and bargain with the enemy—not to fight. This time it was different.

On May 8, Germans surrounded ŻOB headquarters. More than one hundred fighters were trapped inside. The Germans sealed the entrances and pumped gas inside. One of the ŻOB fighters called out, "Let's not fall into their hands alive!" At this, some of the fighters began committing suicide. One of them was Mordecai Anielewicz. Two days later, approximately seventy-five ŻOB survivors slipped into the sewer system of Warsaw to escape.

The Nazis had crushed the uprising. The ghetto was liquidated. It had ceased to exist. But the Jews of Warsaw had upheld the motto:

"To Live With Honor and Die With Honor"

The bodies of Jewish policemen executed by the SS during the
Warsaw ghetto uprising.

53

chapter seven

Those Who Survived

Death tolls within the ghetto walls were high. In the Lodz ghetto, the number was 45,000 out of 200,000—nearly one out of four. In Warsaw, where a total of 470,000 people lived, more than 83,000 died in the ghetto—one out of every five or six. The rate of death was similar in other ghettos, even though they were smaller. Those who managed to survive the horror of the ghettos often did so only to find themselves deported in cattle cars to Nazi death camps.

Looking Back, Looking Ahead

At the camps, teenagers usually stood the best chances of survival. They were young and tougher than the rest—and fiercely determined to live.

In August 1944, Rita Hilton, her mother, and her grandmother were deported to Auschwitz. Rita's grandmother was gassed. Rita and her mother were sent to the Bergen-Belsen concentration camp in Germany, which was liberated by British troops on April 15, 1945. They moved to the United States in May 1946.

Looking back on her Holocaust experience, Rita says her family was the key to her survival and helped her get through the most difficult times.

"The first few years in the ghetto, we had to take care of my grandparents, no matter what. Later I lived with my mother. The times she was sick, I would take care of her. When I was sick, she would take care of me. We looked out for each other."

The emotion that haunts Rita most, more than fifty years later, is anger. "I watch a film or television show about the Holocaust and I say, 'How dare they do that to us! How dare they make us subhumans! What audacity to treat us the way they treated us! I have a deep burning anger of why they did it. What human being has a right to do that to other human beings?"

Irene Weber somehow withstood the extreme deprivation in the Little Fortress at Theresienstadt. The only one of her family to survive the Holocaust, she does not hate. But, she says, she feels "ashamed for the human race." She, too, credits her parents for her survival, even though she was taken from them at an early age. "My parents, the environment I grew up in—I believe it played a very large role."

After the war, Irene was planning to emigrate to Palestine (Israel today), but her future husband would settle nowhere but the United States, so Irene changed her plans. She has never regretted the move.

"This is my country, this is it, and I will fight for it, for my rights in this country. This is the greatest privilege, the greatest gift that this country has given me, the right to fight for my rights. And I wouldn't want to live without it."

Icek Baum, who survived Auschwitz death camp, is haunted by the horror that still stalks many Holocaust survivors. "Sometimes I wake up at night and I say, 'It was impossible. It's a dream. I dreamed about that, but it's impossible that things like that happen in the 20th century.'

"The people in Germany, they are cultivated people. They are organized people—but they are doing things like that. It is something impossible. And nobody, nobody lifted a finger to help. Nobody said one word. And God, where was God?"

Timeline

January 30, 1933	Adolf Hitler is appointed chancellor of Germany.
March 23, 1933	Dachau, the first concentration camp, is built to hold political opponents of Nazis.
April 1, 1933	Nazis proclaim a daylong boycott of Jewish-owned businesses.
July 14, 1933	Nazis outlaw all other political parties in Germany; a law is passed legalizing forced sterilization of Roma and Sinti (Gypsies), mentally and physically disabled Germans, African-Germans, and others.
January 26, 1934	Germany and Poland sign Non-Aggression Pact.
August 1, 1935	"No Jews" signs appear in Germany forbidding Jews from stores, restaurants, places of entertainment, etc.
September 15, 1935	German parliament passes the Nuremberg Laws severely restricting the rights of Jews.
March 13, 1938	Germany annexes Austria.
September 29, 1938	Munich Conference: Britain and France allow Hitler to annex part of Czechoslovakia in order to prevent war.
November 9, 1938	Kristallnacht (looting and vandalism of Jewish homes and businesses and widespread destruction of synagogues) occurs throughout Germany and Austria; 30,000 Jews are sent to Nazi concentration camps.
March 15, 1939	Germany invades all of Czechoslovakia.
August 23, 1939	Germany and Soviet Union sign Non-Aggression Pact.
September 1, 1939	Germany invades western Poland.

September 2, 1939	Great Britain and France declare war on Germany.
September 17, 1939	Soviet Union invades eastern Poland.
Spring 1940	Germany invades Denmark, Norway, Holland, Luxembourg, Belgium, and France.
March 24, 1941	Germany invades North Africa.
April 6, 1941	Germany invades Yugoslavia and Greece.
June 22, 1941	Germany invades western Soviet Union.
July 31, 1941	Reinhard Heydrich appointed to carry out the "Final Solution" (extermination of all European Jews).
Summer 1941	*Einsatzgruppen* (mobile killing squads) begin to massacre Jews in western Soviet Union.
December 7, 1941	Japan bombs Pearl Harbor; United States enters World War II.
January 20, 1942	Wannsee Conference: Nazi leaders meet to design "Final Solution to the Jewish Question."
Spring and Summer 1942	
	Many Polish ghettos emptied; residents deported to death camps.
February 2, 1943	German troops in Stalingrad, Soviet Union, surrender; the Allies begin to win the war.
June 11, 1943	Nazis decide that all ghettos in Poland and Soviet Union are to be emptied and residents deported to death camps.
March 19, 1944	Germany occupies Hungary.
June 6, 1944	D-Day: Normandy Invasion by the Allies.
May 8, 1945	Germany surrenders to the Allies; war ends in Europe.

Glossary

Aktion A Nazi roundup of Jews for deportation to the camps.

Auschwitz The largest of the Nazi death camps, near Cracow, Poland.

concentration camp A camp in which people live in inhumane conditions and may be killed by starvation, exhaustion, disease, torture, or execution.

cyanide A deadly poison that kills quickly after it is swallowed.

death camp A concentration camp where people considered unfit for work or racially undesirable are murdered.

deportation The forced removal of people from one country or area to another.

Final Solution The Nazi plan to murder all the Jews of Europe.

gas chamber A large locked room designed to murder people on a mass scale by the use of the poison gas Zyklon B.

Gentile A non-Jewish person.

Gestapo The Nazis' secret state police.

ghetto A part of a city set aside by the Nazis to contain only Jews. Ghettos were heavily guarded and lacking in food, water, heat, housing, and health care.

Hitler Youth A Nazi youth group, in which boys were trained to believe the Nazi ideology and prepared to become soldiers.

Holocaust The extermination of six million Jews and millions of others during World War II.

Kristallnacht Meaning the "night of broken glass," November 9, 1938, was a government-sponsored attack on Jews, resulting in the destruction of Jewish-owned businesses and synagogues.

liquidation To clear out or empty an area of people, usually by deportation or execution.

Nazis The political party that ruled in Germany (1933–1945); full name: National Socialist German Workers' Party.

rations The amount of food people are allowed for a specified period during wartime.

Resistance Organized opposition, often in secret, to the ruling political party or leader.

SS (Schutzstaffeln, or "protection squads") The Nazis' special security forces.

Theresienstadt A ghetto and concentration camp in the town of Terezin, Czechoslovakia.

typhus A highly contagious disease that is fatal if not treated. Many concentration camp prisoners died from typhus during the Holocaust.

ŻOB (Żydowska Organizacja Bojowa, or "Jewish Combat Organization") A Jewish Resistance group in the Warsaw ghetto that briefly fought off German troops during April and May of 1943.

For Further Reading

Altschuler, David A. *Hitler's War Against the Jews.* West Orange, NJ: Behrman House, 1978.

Drucker, Malka, and Michael Halperin. *Jacob's Rescue: A Holocaust Story.* New York: Bantam Doubleday Dell, 1993.

Eisenberg, Azriel. *The Lost Generation: Children in the Holocaust.* New York: Pilgrim Press, 1982.

Eliach, Yaffa. *Hasidic Tales of the Holocaust.* New York: Random House, 1988.

Frank, Anne. *Diary of a Young Girl: The Definitive Edition.* New York: Doubleday, 1995.

Holliday, Laurel. *Children in the Holocaust and World War II: Their Secret Diaries.* New York: Washington Square Press, 1994.

Klein, Gerda. *All but My Life.* New York: Hill & Wang, 1995.

Laird, Christa. *Shadow of the Wall.* New York: Greenwillow, 1989.

Orlev, Uri. *The Man from the Other Side.* Boston: Houghton Mifflin, 1991.

Rochman, Hazel, and Darlene Z. McCampbell, eds. *Bearing Witness: Stories of the Holocaust.* New York: Orchard Books Watts, 1995.

Volavková, Hana, ed. *I Never Saw Another Butterfly: Children's Drawings and Poems from Terezin Concentration Camp.* New York: Shocken Books, 1994.

For Advanced Readers

Bernheim, Mark. *Father of the Orphans: The Story of Janusz Korczak.* New York: Lodestar Books, 1989.

Dwork, Deborah. *Children with a Star.* New Haven, CT: Yale University Press, 1991.

Edelheit, Abraham J., and Herschel Edelheit. *History of the Holocaust: A Handbook and Dictionary.* Boulder, CO: Westview Press, 1994.

Gilbert, Martin. *The Holocaust: A History of the Jews of Europe During the Second World War.* New York: Henry Holt & Co., 1985.

Wiesel, Elie. *Night.* New York: Bantam Books, 1982.

Videos

Korczak
This film dramatizes the life story of Janusz Korczak, the brave doctor who ran the orphanage in the Warsaw ghetto. When the orphans were deported and sent to the death camps, Korczak refused to leave them, and they went to their deaths together. (Available from New York Films Video, 16 West 61st Street, New York, NY 10023; (212) 247-6110.

Lodz Ghetto
The Lodz ghetto, in Lodz, Poland, was one of the largest ghettos, and one of the last to be liquidated. This documentary uses slides, photographs, and film footage to describe the life and death of the ghetto. (Available from Alan Adelson, Jewish Heritage Project, Inc., 150 Franklin Street, #1W, New York, NY 10003; (212) 925-9067.)

The Warsaw Ghetto
This documentary uses film footage made by the Nazis. It details the history of the Warsaw ghetto, from its creation to its liquidation, including the brave, tragic uprising. (Available from Zenger Video, P. O. Box 802, Culver City, CA 90232-0802; (800) 421-4246.)

Partisans of Vilna
Forty survivors of the ghetto in Vilna, Lithuania, tell their stories. (Available from National Center for Jewish Films, Brandeis University, Lown 102, MS053, Waltham, MA 02454; (781) 899-7044.)

Web Sites

Anti-Defamation League—Braun Holocaust Institute
http://www.adl.org/Braun/braun.htm

Cybrary of the Holocaust
http://www.remember.org

Holocaust Education and Memorial Centre of Toronto
http://www.feduja.org

Museum of Tolerance
www.wiesenthal.com/mot/index.html

United States Holocaust Memorial Museum
http://www.ushmm.org/index.html

Yad Vashem
http://www.yad-vashem.org.il

Index

About the Author

Eleanor H. Ayer wrote more than 50 books for children and young adults on a wide range of topics including the Holocaust, World War II, and social issues Her dedication as an author and her interest in children and young adults are reflected in the many awards her books have received. Mrs. Ayer earned a master's degree in literacy journalism from Syracuse University. For the last 25 years, she made her home in Frederick, Colorado, with her husband and two sons. Tragically, in June 1998, she was fatally injured in an automobile accident.

About the Series Editor

Yaffa Eliach is Professor of History and Literature in the Department of Judaic Studies at Brooklyn College. She founded and directed the Center for Holocaust Studies and created the Tower of Life exhibit at the U.S. Holocaust Memorial Museum. Professor Eliach's book *There Once Was a World: A Nine Hundred Year Chronicle of the Shtetl of Eishyshok;* was a finalist for the 1998 National Book Award for Nonfiction. She is also the author of *Hasidic Tales of the Holocaust; We Were Children Just Like You;* and *The Liberators: Eyewitness Accounts of the Liberation of Concentration Camps.*

Photo Credits

Cover photo, pp. 6, 27, 28, 32 © Yad Vashem Photo Archives, courtesy of the United States Holocaust Memorial Museum (USHMM) Photo Archives; pp. 8-9 © Archiwum Akt Nowych, courtesy of USHMM Photo Archives; pp. 10, 12, 38 © Bildarchiv Preussischer Kulturbesitz, courtesy of USHMM Photo Archives; p. 11 © Dokumentationsarchiv des Osterreichischen Widerstandes, courtesy of USHMM Photo Archives; pp. 12 (background), 23, 29 © YIVO Institute for Jewish Research, courtesy of USHMM Photo Archives; p. 15 © Jack J. Silverstein, courtesy of USHMM Photo Archives; pp. 16-17 © Bundesarchiv, courtesy of USHMM Photo Archives, p. 19 Zydowski Instytut Historyczny Instytut Naukowo-Badawczy, courtesy of USHMM Photo Archives; p. 21, 33, 34-35, 47 © Beit Lohamei Haghettaot, courtesy of USHMM Photo Archives; p. 22 © Archives of Mechanical Documentation, courtesy of USHMM Photo Archives; p. 25 © Guenther Schwarberg, courtesy of USHMM Photo Archives; p. 31 © Jerzy Tomaszewski, courtesy of USHMM Photo Archives; pp. 36-37, 39, 40-41, 42-43 © Jewish Museum in Prague; p. 45 © Terezin Memorial Museum, courtesy of USHMM Photo Archives; p. 48 © 1998 PhotoDisc, Inc.; p. 50 © Main Commission for the Investigation of Nazi War Crimes, courtesy of USHMM Photo Archives; p. 51 © National Archives, courtesy of USHMM Photo Archives; p. 53 © Leopold Page Photographic Collection, courtesy of USHMM Photo Archives.

Series Design
Kim Sonsky

Layout
Laura Murawski